CONTENTS

Glossary words defined on p. 31 are in **bold** the first time they appear in the text.

WAR CORRESPONDENT

Most of us don't think about danger when we go to work. There are some jobs, however, in which danger is an everyday reality. Soldiers, police officers, and fighter pilots: all of these people go into dangerous situations to do their jobs. So do war correspondents. A war correspondent is a journalist who reports from areas of conflict to television and radio stations, newspapers and magazines, and websites.

▼ **Barbara Starr is a war and military correspondent for the TV news network CNN. She is seen here interviewing U.S. General Peter Pace in a conflict zone in Iraq.**

The World's MOST DANGEROUS Jobs

War Correspondents

By Sabrina Crewe

CRABTREE
Publishing Company
www.crabtreebooks.com

The World's **MOST DANGEROUS** Jobs

This book is dedicated to Marie Colvin, who helped the author with this book and who was killed in Homs, Syria, on February 22, 2012, doing the job she loved.

Author: Sabrina Crewe
Managing editor: Paul Humphrey
Editorial director: Kathy Middleton
Editors: James Nixon, Adrianna Morganelli
Proofreader: Rachel Eagen
Series Design: Elaine Wilkinson
Page Design: sprout.uk.com
Cover design: Margaret Salter
Production coordinator: Margaret Salter
Prepress technician: Margaret Salter
Print coordinator: Katherine Berti

Photo credits:
Daniel Pearl Foundation: page 18
Getty Images: pages 11 (Jaafar Ashtiyeh/AFP), 14 (Eric Feferberg/AFP), 24 (Gwenn Dubourthoumieu/AFP), 25 (STRINGER/AFP), 26 (Mauricio Lima/AFP)
Photoshot: pages 6 (Jason Howe/WpN), 8 (WpN/UPPA), 9 (WpN/UPPA), 13 (WpN/UPPA), 15 (Jason Howe/WpN), 21 (UPPA), 28 (Gary Lee/UPPA)
Thinkstock: iStockphoto: cover (bottom)
U.S. Army: cover (top), page 4 (AF Staff Sgt. D. Myles Cullen), 16–17 (AF Staff Sgt. Brian Ferguson), 29 (Pfc. Gregory Gieske)
Wikipedia: page 27 (Al Jazeera)

COVER STORY

◀ **COVER (top) – Barbara Starr, a war and military correspondent, interviews U.S. General Peter Pace in a conflict zone in Iraq.**

◀ **COVER (bottom) – A camouflaged war photographer sets up for a picture.**

PAGE 1 – A bomb explodes next to the U.S. Army truck in which New York Times reporter John Burns is traveling.

Library and Archives Canada Cataloguing in Publication

Crewe, Sabrina
War correspondents / Sabrina Crewe.

(The world's most dangerous jobs)
Includes index.
Issued also in electronic format.
ISBN 978-0-7787-5103-8 (bound).--ISBN 978-0-7787-5117-5 (pbk.)

1. War correspondents--Juvenile literature. 2. War--Press coverage--Juvenile literature. I. Title. II. Series: World's most dangerous jobs

PN4823.C73 2012 j070.4'333092 C2012-901575-X

Library of Congress Cataloging-in-Publication Data

Crewe, Sabrina.
War correspondents / Sabrina Crewe.
p. cm. -- (The world's most dangerous jobs)
Includes index.
ISBN 978-0-7787-5103-8 (reinforced library binding : alk. paper) -- ISBN 978-0-7787-5117-5 (pbk. : alk. paper) -- ISBN 978-1-4271-8070-4 (electronic pdf) -- ISBN 978-1-4271-8074-2 (electronic html)
1. War correspondents--Juvenile literature. 2. War--Press coverage--Juvenile literature. I. Title.

PN4823.C74 2012
070.4'333092--dc23

2012008527

Crabtree Publishing Company
www.crabtreebooks.com 1-800-387-7650

Printed in Canada/042012/KR20120316

 In Canada: We acknowledge the financial support of the Government of Canada through the Canada Book Fund for our publishing activities.

Published in Canada
Crabtree Publishing
616 Welland Ave.
St. Catharines, Ontario
L2M 5V6

Published in the United States
Crabtree Publishing
PMB 59051
350 Fifth Avenue, 59th Floor
New York, New York 10118

Published in the United Kingdom
Crabtree Publishing
Maritime House
Basin Road North, Hove
BN41 1WR

Published in Australia
Crabtree Publishing
3 Charles Street
Coburg North
VIC 3058

War correspondents may work for large organizations and travel with TV crews. Or, they may enter dangerous war zones alone to find a story and capture images that a news station will want. They may be **embedded**—working alongside fighting forces in the heart of a battlefield. Or they may live among civilians, looking for the human stories behind the war.

Whether they work alone or as part of a team, war correspondents have to go to the most dangerous places in the world. These are the places where people are fighting with lethal weapons, bombs are exploding, and the lives of journalists are in constant danger. They risk capture, arrest, injury, death, and **trauma**.

"Covering war and scores of human tragedies... is a bit like exposing oneself to radiation... Journalists can suffer devastating psychological effects from even a single traumatic event, just as soldiers and emergency workers can."

Lawrence Sheets, former war reporter

"For us, war is a blur, something not to fight but to report and to survive; we are **civilians** in conflict more often with ourselves, our distant employers, our unseen audiences. War rages all around us; war itself is neutral; it does not care whether we live or die."

Tony Maniaty, former Australian television journalist

THE DEMAND FOR DANGER

In recent years, there has been huge growth in the television news industry. Several news stations broadcast 24 hours a day. This creates a constant demand for "new" news. The news stations want facts and updates. But they also want **sensationalism**, human stories, and drama.

The demand for live reports and frequent updates has had an effect on war reporting. Correspondents put themselves at risk to satisfy the need for dangerous and shocking reports and images.

"In the world of 24/7 breaking news it is all about being live, as it happens, at the scene, up to the minute. Exciting, breathless and edgy reporting from the **frontline** as the bullets and the rocket-propelled grenades fly. Get that sound. Get that picture. Get it all. Because if we don't the opposition will."

Mark Austin, U.K. news anchor

A handful of war correspondents become familiar faces on the evening news. They may become celebrities, even hosting their own TV shows.

The Internet has created even more demand for information. News websites are constantly updated with breaking news from war zones. The Internet also gives opportunities to **amateur** correspondents. People who find themselves in the middle of a conflict often record images on their cell phones. They can post these images on websites to be seen by millions of people.

"A really good day for us is probably the worst day or last day of life for somebody who we're dealing with."

Jeremy Bowen, BBC war correspondent

◀ Meeting the demand for danger is part of the job. This photo of *New York Times* reporter John Burns was taken moments after a bomb exploded next to the U.S. Army truck in which he was traveling.

PROFILE OF A CORRESPONDENT

What kind of person makes a good war correspondent? Like all journalists, war correspondents need to be curious about the world around them. They should have an interest in world affairs, politics, and conflict. Reporters are eager to seek out information and communicate it to other people.

"The men and women who cover wars and conflicts around the globe are almost uniformly tough (at least outwardly), driven, and obsessed with their jobs."

Mark Austin, U.K. news anchor

◄ These members of a TV news crew run to keep up with events. War correspondents and their teams must always be ready to capture an image or a story.

Journalists need to communicate well verbally and in writing. They need to be accurate in their fact gathering and truthful in what they write or say. War correspondents must try hard not to be **biased** in their reporting.

Reporters from the battlefield will live in uncomfortable, unsafe places, and they must be ready to face difficulties and danger. It is important for a war correspondent to be cool under pressure.

> "Who had we been before we became war correspondents? Scholars, researchers, musicians, poets—I don't know. But war correspondents we all had become, and now we all thrived on it, courting death just to try and keep feeling a little bit alive."
>
> **Thomas Goltz, author and journalist**

◄ **Reporters have to be clear communicators to explain complex events to their audiences and readers.**

TRAINING FOR THE JOB

Even if you fit the profile of a good war correspondent, you will still need training. Journalism is a skill that must be learned and practiced. It is hard to get a job in journalism without a college degree. Any degree would be useful because journalists have to write about all kinds of subjects. A degree that combines journalism or communications with political science or a foreign language would give a future war correspondent a head start.

After college, most reporters start careers at a local newspaper or in local radio or television. This can lead to a job with a national newspaper or television network. Eventually, by being in the right place at the right time, a journalist can get a placement overseas.

Some extra skills will help get a hopeful war correspondent into a conflict zone. Training as a **videographer** is an advantage for TV reporters. The Canadian Defence & Foreign Affairs Institute (CDFAI) runs courses for reporters interested in military journalism. Students learn military theory and make field visits to army units.

Hostile environment training for aspiring journalists is also a plus. News organizations want to know that their reporters can handle themselves in dangerous situations.

◀ This TV news crew take cover behind a vehicle while caught in crossfire in the conflict between Israel and Palestine.

"If you're going to hang out with the war jocks, get in shape. No one expects you to qualify for Special Forces school, but if you're an overweight chain-smoker, you're not going to inspire a lot of confidence in the infantry unit you want to tag along with, and you're likely to get left back at base (for your own good, and theirs)."

Teru Kuwayama, photographer

BEING PREPARED: TECHNOLOGY AND EQUIPMENT

According to veteran correspondent Joe Galloway, no journalist should enter a war zone without the following items:

- First aid supplies and medicines, especially antibiotics
- A good flashlight, a small radio, and a camera
- Plastic bags to wrap equipment in
- A "big neckerchief" (a bandana or other handkerchief) to protect mouth from sand and neck from sunburn
- Water, canteen cup, and fuel bars to heat water
- A Swiss Army knife, earplugs, and a compass
- Gloves, hiking boots, fleece, and a waterproof poncho

War correspondents generally wear wool or cotton clothing. They avoid synthetic fabrics that could melt into their skin in an explosion or fire. Journalists in war zones also wear body armor and protective helmets.

Armor and helmets are made of Kevlar, a material that is five times stronger than steel. Kevlar can resist bullets, blades, and heat. It has saved many lives.

War correspondents depend on their computers to record news and send stories. Using a laptop, **satellite phone**, and video camera, reporters can send in stories from anywhere in the world. In an instant, they can beam written reports, photos, sound, and moving images from the battlefield to a newsroom thousands of miles away.

When a reporter works with a camera crew, the newsgathering equipment is bigger and more complicated. A cameraperson will carry a large camera along with a tripod, lenses, batteries, lights, and microphones.

"There is no special protection for journalists who travel with the American or Iraqi military. Journalists wear the same Kevlar helmets and protective vests the troops wear but parts of the body are always exposed. You feel relatively secure in American Humvees that have proper armor, combat locks and a gunner always on lookout. Iraqi military vehicles do not always have similar protection."

Aaron Katersky, ABC News reporter

▼ These TV news team members are wearing protective vests.

EMBEDDED

War correspondents are special reporters who may accompany military units into battle. From the frontline, reporters can truly describe the experience of war.

When the United States went to war in Iraq in 2003, many journalists and photographers went, too. They lived with military units and reported from the soldiers' point of view. War correspondents who were placed in a military unit to live alongside soldiers became known as embedded journalists. Today, war correspondents are embedded with military forces and rebel groups in conflicts all over the world.

▲ Embedded photographers in Iraq capture U.S. soldiers in action during an attack by Iraqis.

Being embedded gives war correspondents a chance to convey what war really feels like. When they are embedded, journalists must agree not to report **classified** information or anything else that would endanger lives. Being embedded exposes reporters to the same dangers that troops face. There is no special protection for journalists. These dangers include being blown up by grenades, being shot at, and being bombed.

"Be careful what opportunities you accept. Once you are accepted in any unit you will get offers to "come on along with us." Find out all the info you can about their mission and decide accordingly. A small unit foot patrol on a 15-mile night mission including a river crossing? Accept only those things you are physically capable of doing and ask yourself if you will get a story that is worth the risk. Do not touch or move anything strange on the battlefield. It will likely blow up in your face."

Joseph Galloway, war correspondent

▼ A journalist embedded with the U.S. military, wades ashore with troops during a military operation along the Euphrates River in Iraq.

DEADLY EXPLOSIONS

Not all wars and conflicts have clear battlefields. There may be no frontline and, therefore, no safe zone either. The risks are hard to see when you can't tell who or where your enemy is. This is the case with **terrorist** activities.

Insurgents are people who rise up against the government. Terrorists are people who use violence and threats to gain political control or attention. In many conflict zones, the biggest danger is a surprise attack by insurgents or terrorists.

▼ An IED is detonated during a training scenario at the National Training Center in California.

These attacks come in several deadly forms. One of the most lethal is the improvised explosive device (IED). IEDs are homemade explosives, and they are often planted in innocent-looking vehicles. An IED can be detonated by a remote control device, a tripwire, or even a cell phone.

Suicide bombers use another kind of IED. They wear vests loaded with explosives that they detonate with a trigger. Suicide bombers kill themselves and kill or injure those around them. These terrorists have claimed the lives of journalists working in conflict zones.

"On 7th of February (2011), whilst on patrol in Afghanistan with the 1st Squadron, 75th Cavalry Regiment, U.S. Army, I stepped on an IED. Moments after the explosion I remember doing a stock check on my body; I was aware my eyes, right hand and mind were all in order, there was nothing to stop me being what I am, a photographer. In some ways my world changed forever on that day, the loss of three limbs meant life would naturally be harder, but in other ways nothing changed. Since the incident I've heard of myself referred to as a victim of the war. I am nothing of the sort. I knew the risks being a photographer entailed, but taking these photographs somehow felt important and I am honored to do it."

Giles Duley, British photojournalist

CAPTURE

American, Canadian, and British reporters face added dangers in some war and conflict zones. They have been captured and held hostage because they are Westerners, or because they are well known, or both. If someone with a famous face or name is captured, it can attract a huge amount of publicity.

Usually, a foreign reporter held by **militia** or other forces is soon released. But some have not been so lucky. They have been used to grab attention for terrorists' political causes. Some war correspondents and other journalists in conflict zones have been held for months or years. A few have been tortured and even put to death.

Daniel Pearl was investigating the war on terror in Pakistan in January 2002 when he was captured. The captors wanted the United States to release suspected terrorists in exchange for Pearl's life. Their message said: "We give you one more day. If America will not meet our demands we will kill Daniel. Then this cycle will continue and no American journalist could enter Pakistan." For a few weeks, there was no news. Then, on February 21, Pearl's murder was confirmed. The terrorists made a video of his execution to prove he was dead.

◀ **Daniel Pearl was 38 years old when he was killed while working in Pakistan.**

▶ **Writer and filmmaker Robert Young Pelton, shown here with his captors, was kidnapped in Colombia by rebel forces. His captors were members of a violent death squad.**

Journalist Robert Young Pelton

stumbled into a paramilitaries' search-and-destroy mission and was captured. After his release he said:

> "Every hour is a new hour when you're held at gunpoint. At times, the mood was relaxed, but overall, it was very stressful. We didn't know whether we were going to be killed or released, whether our captors would be attacked."

WOMEN IN THE WAR ZONE

In some parts of the world, female war correspondents face extra dangers. Several conflicts that correspondents are covering today are in countries where women do not have equal rights. They are not allowed to work or wear certain clothes. Women reporters, therefore, are treated with hostility.

In February 2011, CBS foreign correspondent Lara Logan was in Egypt to report on events following a popular **uprising** against the government. She was surrounded by a hostile crowd in Tahrir Square in the center of the Egyptian capital of Cairo. According to CBS News, Logan "suffered a brutal, sustained sexual assault and beating before being saved by a group of women and an estimated 20 Egyptian soldiers."

"These days, there are more women writing and broadcasting about war so the bad guys are getting used to us."

***Marie Colvin, foreign correspondent**

**Marie Colvin was tragically killed in February 2012 while covering the uprising in Syria.*

"When I started out, there was just me so it was easier. When I went to a war zone there were lots of men with guns, and when they saw a woman they just thought I was stupid or somebody's sister so they completely underestimated me. It didn't bother me what they thought of me. I could ask my questions, and write my notes, and take my photos and come up with a really good story.

Sometimes it is more difficult being a woman. I was in Tahrir Square just a week ago and I had men groping me, along with the tear gas being fired and the rubber bullets and live ammunition. So it is one more risk. But I love the job and I think I can make a difference in the world, bearing witness to the atrocities and heroism of war, in equal measure. So I will soldier on."

Marie Colvin, foreign correspondent

▼ In some countries, it can be easier for women caught in conflicts to talk to female reporters. Marie Colvin (right) is interviewing an Iraqi women who fled with her children from the fighting.

GOING ALONE

Today's technology gives war correspondents great independence. Equipped with a small digital video camera and a laptop, a solo reporter can become a one-person news team. Many solo reporters are **freelance**—working for themselves and selling their stories and images to a number of news organizations.

Large news organizations cannot always send a news team into a war zone. Networks use freelancers, especially locals, in areas where they consider it too dangerous to send their own staff. This means solo reporters do not have the support of a team or a network behind them. If they are not embedded, they have no military protection either.

Kevin Sites was one of the first Internet-only correspondents to cover international conflicts. Sites was an Internet **blogger** and a news correspondent for Yahoo! In 2005, he set out on a year-long journey to cover every war zone in the world. Sites sometimes reported news that wasn't covered on TV and in newspapers. He used his reports to call public attention to the suffering caused by wars.

"When I go in to a place, I draw less attention by myself than I would if I had four people with me."

Kevin Sites

◀ **Kevin Sites films a story for his online project "In the Hot Zone." Every day, he sent in videos, photos, and stories that several million people could view on the Internet.**

"To reach the status of war reporter, you had to put in years of hard grind, and when you finally flew off to war, your entourage included a camera person, a sound person and a dozen metal boxes of gear. Today, my students can—and some do—circumvent all that rigmarole by walking around the corner, buying a laptop and HD camera and a cheap air ticket to Kabul, and two days later be filming—alone, unsupported—on the frontline."

Tony Maniaty, former Australian television journalist

HIDDEN WARS

War correspondents head into danger to get the best possible stories and pictures for their news organizations. But many face danger for another reason. They believe it is important to witness and report on human suffering.

These journalists say it is their job to expose injustice and violence that harms innocent people. They may work in places where the powers on either side of a conflict want to keep reporters away.

"We can and do make a difference in exposing the horrors of war and especially the atrocities that befall civilians."

Marie Colvin, foreign correspondent

▼ In 2011, reporters tried to call attention to the killings in the Democratic Republic of Congo by the security forces of President Joseph Kabila.

"They (war correspondents) tend to haunt wretched, nasty places that the civilized world doesn't care about: Sierra Leone, the Democratic Republic of Congo. They go there in hopes of forcing the world to pay attention, and most of the time the world is indifferent."

David Plotz, editor of Slate.com

Many journalists working in their native countries put themselves in danger just by reporting the truth. Some of these local reporters are among the bravest. In Somalia, radio journalists have kept broadcasting in their war-torn country even though their reports anger government and rebel forces. The journalists want people to know about the civil war in their country. Several of them have been killed by forces who do not want the journalists' reports heard.

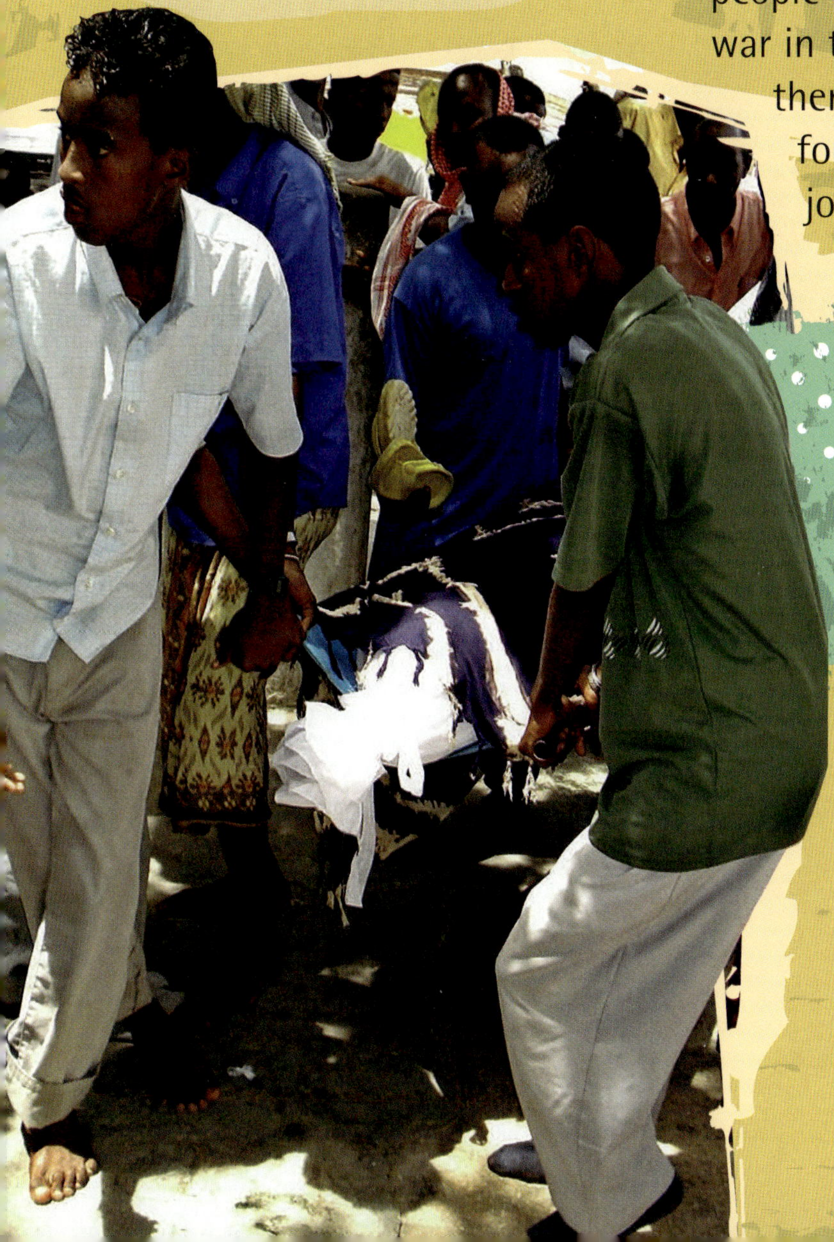

Political or military groups may threaten, arrest, or harm foreign and local reporters.

◄ Mahad Ahmed Elmi was shot and killed on his way to work at the Horn Afrik radio station in Somalia in 2007. The station's owner, Ali Iman Sharmake, was killed when his car exploded just hours later.

> "Journalists covering combat shoulder great responsibilities and face difficult choices. Sometimes they pay the ultimate price... it has never been more dangerous to be a war correspondent, because the journalist in the combat zone has become a prime target."

Marie Colvin, foreign correspondent

▼ Security forces search for survivors after suicide bombers detonated explosives near the Al Hamra Hotel in Baghdad, Iraq. The hotel was used by foreign correspondents.

CASUALTIES

Today, many war correspondents receive safety training before they go on assignment. In spite of this training, war correspondents sometimes lose their lives in the course of their jobs.

In 2011, the Committee to Protect Journalists recorded fifteen journalists killed on dangerous assignments and eight journalists killed in crossfire or combat.

Afghanistan has claimed the lives of several war correspondents. Canadian war correspondent Michelle Lang (right) of the *Calgary Herald* was killed in Afghanistan in 2009. She was traveling in a military convoy with Canadian troops when the convoy was hit by a roadside bomb. Rupert Hamer, reporter for the U.K.'s *Sunday Mirror* was embedded with U.S. Marines in 2010. He also died in a military vehicle targeted by an IED.

"A few weeks ago I traveled with a cameraman to Mogadishu in Somalia—possibly one of the most dangerous capital cities in the world right now. We knew that as Westerners we ran a considerable risk of kidnap or worse. We knew also that as Western journalists we were particularly juicy targets for the Islamist militants or the gangs linked to them. We were determined to go to see for ourselves what was going on there."

Mark Austin, U.K. news anchor

BATTLE SCARS

Some war correspondents wear their battle scars on the outside. The BBC's Frank Gardner was paralyzed after a terrorist attack and now reports from his wheelchair. American reporter, Marie Colvin of The Sunday Times, sported an eye patch after she was shot while working in Sri Lanka. Colvin lost sight in her left eye from this attack. In February, 2012, Colvin was killed while on assignment in Syria.

Not all the dangers of being a war correspondent are physical, however. Other reporters' lives are affected forever by their experiences, even if they are not injured.

They have emotional scars. Like soldiers, war correspondents can develop post-traumatic stress disorder (PTSD). This condition can strike people exposed to trauma or disaster. PTSD has many symptoms. It can cause nightmares, anxiety, anger, and depression.

► Frank Gardner goes to Buckingham Palace to be honored by Queen Elizabeth II for his services to journalism.

In the end, many war correspondents just get tired—both of the danger and of witnessing suffering and death. Some go home to write about other things. Others work to help the victims of war and conflict in whatever way they can.

> "There is no way I can prepare someone who has never witnessed combat for the shock of the first sight of a badly wounded soldier, screaming in pain, begging for his mother. Or the sight of the face of a young soldier in death... a soldier of either side. You will learn to process the images and move on and do your job. But what you see in battle will never leave you."
>
> **Joseph Galloway, war correspondent**

IT'S A FACT!

Between 1992 and 2012, over 160 journalists are reported to have died in combat or crossfire. Around eighty-five percent of those were war correspondents.

Henry Crabb Robinson was an early war correspondent, writing about the Napoleonic Wars in the early 1800s for *The Times* newspaper of London. William Howard Russell was the first well-known correspondent. He covered several famous battles during the Crimean War, including the famous Charge of the Light Brigade in 1854.

Hostile Environment and **First Aid Training** (HEFAT) is mandatory for all BBC journalists going to war zones. Trainees learn everything from how to use chemical warfare protection gear to what to do during a kidnapping.

Former war correspondent Anderson Cooper is now a news anchor, TV host, and major celebrity earning millions of dollars a year.

War Correspondents Online

The Association for Military Journalists: http://militaryreporters.org/

Committee to Protect Journalists: http://cpj.org/

The Rory Peck Trust: http://www.rorypecktrust.org/

GLOSSARY

amateur A person who is not a professional or expert

biased Holding a personal view that influences one's outlook or presentation of facts

blogger A person who makes regular entries on a personal website with news or opinions or both

civilians People who are not members of any military force

classified Officially secret and only available to a certain group of people

embedded Firmly fixed in place

freelance Working for yourself, selling a service to a variety of companies

frontline The place where a battlefield or zone of conflict begins

Hostile Environment and First Aid Training Safety training that prepares people to go into dangerous places and situations

insurgents People who resist government or other authority, often by fighting

militia A military force that is not the official army of a nation

satellite phone A type of mobile phone that transmits and receives from a space satellite and so works in places where there are no communications towers to transmit signals

sensationalism The process of creating drama or making events seem exciting to attract an audience

terrorist A person who tries to frighten people or governments by using violence or the threat of violence

trauma An incident that causes terrible emotional or physical distress or injury

uprising A protest movement or demonstration by a large number of people against a ruling power. Sometimes uprisings lead to civil war or to the overthrow of a government

videographer Person who uses a video camera

INDEX